Secret to long lasting relationship: How to stay long with your partner

Table of content

INTRODUCTION.

Everyone desires a butterflies-in-your-stomach still-in-love-50-years-later reasonably love. But, supported the analysis of unsuccessful relationships and marriages, not several areas willing to place within the work to accomplish this type of affection. Relationships area unit exertions. Even the foremost prosperous couples admit that keeping their love alive isn't straightforward.[1] but, if you're willing to put in the effort, you'll build a long relationship.

Chapter one

Communication

Practice active listening.

This means making ready to pay attention to listen to the message of your partner and to not prepare your defense. notice a time and place wherever you'll be while not distractions and focus solely on what your partner is expressing. attempt to put aside your negative perceptions concerning their actions or motives therefore you'll concentrate on the speech in real time.

Orient towards your partner. build eye contact. Nod your head once you agree and show you're attentive. Once they end speaking, paraphrase what was the same as "What I detected you say was that..." and raise any inquiries to clarify whether or not you bought the proper message "Am I right in thinking you are feeling like...?"

Be aware of the nonverbal signs in addition to what's the same aloud. will the message your partner is sharing with you line up with the nonverbal cues? conjointly, explore for signs of tension or frustration. Balled fists, crossed arms, or frowns might demonstrate that the opposite person desires an occasion or is just too upset to resolve any problems at once.

Though it's going to appear obvious, do not be glancing at your phone, scrolling through social media, or electronic communication individuals. This shows that you just are totally targeted and being attentive to the person ahead of you.

Use "I" Statements.

Communication isn't concerning blame, it's concerning responsibility. "I" statements begin with however you're feeling concerning the behavior or action of your partner. It means that you're taking possession of your feelings and conjointly counsel the way to boost the behavior. the main focus isn't to inform your partner the action is dangerous, simply to share your own expertise.

"You" statements often blame the opposite person. Avoid creating these sorts of statements. they'll sound like "You Pine Tree Stateasure} forever creating massive purchases while not asking me first!"

An example of associate "I" statement is also "I feel confused after you create massive purchases while not Pine Tree State as a result of i assumed we have a tendency to in agreement to travel along. From now on, I might prefer to be enclosed in these purchases."

Use a soft, heat tone once speaking.

Your relationship ought to be supported by mutual respect and love, not fear. A soft voice reflects the love, compassion and understanding that's missing from yelling. Meet your partner's eyes and speak from an area of affection and understanding. Disagreements don't need anger and yelling to resolve.

If lovesome names are unremarkably utilized in your relationship, you'll be able to use such names to point out that you just still look after your partner even throughout a disagreement. spoken communication things like "What does one assume, dear?" or "I'm sorry I frustrated you, baby. however am i able to create things right?" might facilitate to ease the strain.

Basic because it appears, conjointly confirm that you just maintain eye contact.

Be respectful to your partner forever.

Save harsh words, even throughout arguments. You can't take back what's been the same. After you say one thing hurtful to your partner you send the message that a disagreement is love a war. you're on an equivalent aspect. keep that in mind.

To prevent voice communication nasty things and getting trapped in anger, several couples use a "24 hour" rule. During this situation, if things get too heated, they table the discussion for twenty-four hours therefore each party quiets down and an area unit is ready to speak. it's pretty rare to seek out a discussion that can't look ahead to a cooling down amount if want be.

Chapter two

Conflict Resolution.

Discuss problems directly rather than let them grow in size.
It is a relationship story in which a solid relationship doesn't need work. Be ready to place the ad. you'll accomplish this by addressing any issues along with your partner before they rear their ugly heads.
For example, you notice your partner retreating extra money out of a shared account than usual. rather than building a case over time, you may address the difficulty right off by the expression "I detected you've been needing extra money lately. will we have to change our budget to account for this?"
You will ne'er be excellent, nor are you able to expect this from a partner. there'll perpetually be problems that come back up and will|you'll|you'll be able to} either learn to treat

them as you'd the other obstacle otherwise you can hide them till they balloon into an enormous downside.

Make a commitment to carry a weekly arrival within which either of you'll cite any problems you've got on your chest. human action issues with the concept of grappling them as presently as they are available up helps you determine a powerful foundation.

Make sure that you just attempt to follow through with no matter what you 2 say and choose over the course of your oral communication. Plans are solely helpful if they are carried out!

Be willing to compromise.

Pick your battles showing wisdom. Not each issue has to be converted into a battle. there'll be some that require to be talked out, others that go unstated and eventually some that simply find yourself not being necessary compared to what you gain from the connection.[9]

Compromising could embody writing out an execs and cons list to points of disagreement and talking through the list objectively. Talking aloud could clearly imply that selection is mutualist. It conjointly means that finding the way that each of you'll have your desires met while not jeopardizing the wants of the opposite.

Another approach you'll compromise is doing things one person's way on just one occasion then prove the opposite person's opinion succeeding time. For instance, you will watch one person's favorite pic one night and therefore the alternative person's prime will decide the succeeding night.

Before you discover yourself waging war against your partner a couple of little issue, assess however necessary the matter actually is to the happiness and growth of your relationship. If it’s actually not a giant deal, move on.

Work through issues as a team.

Relationships are a unit concerning the "we" and not the "I" or "you". target honest communication to figure through issues beside areas for each of you to provide and take. Learn from each other rather than operating against each other.

For example, if you would like a total of cash to acquire a giant purchase, you'll be able to sit down and notice ways for each of you to contribute. every of you'll be able to place cash into savings for a span of your time, or crop on non-essential expenses.

Using terms like "we" as in "We can get through this" or "us" as in "Let U.S. make out an answer together" facilitate fostering a cooperation approach.

Every relationship comes with ups and downs. after you encounter a difficulty, bear it logically and objectively and build a call supported the mutual well-being of each partners

Make your values and desires identified to your partner.

Be sure to obviously outline what you would like from a partner and what you propose to provide to your partner. Follow through on your obligations to your partner and speak up after they are not doing constant during a constructive manner.

It is a story that you just don't have to be compelled to tell your partner what you are worth and want. you're mistaken to assume that just because your partner loves you, they ought to recognize what you would like. Mind reading is not possible and therefore the expectation of it simply hinders your growth.

Communicate your wishes just by oral communication one thing to the impact of "Charity is absolutely vital to Pine Tree State. What will we tend to do to honor that moving forward?"

Get on an identical page regarding finances.

This is one space that may be terribly dangerous if you ignore it till it becomes a much bigger issue. check that you share monetary values too soon within the relationship. If you would like to save lots for the longer term whereas your partner lives for the instant, this could not find yourself lasting long run.

Sit down and discuss wherever each of you stand financially. produce a budget if you reside beneath an identical roof. seek advice from a monetary counselor if you have got hassle seeing eye-to-eye.

Chapter three

Healthy Habits

Continue to demonstrate honesty and build trust.

This includes giving your partner a constant level of respect and a focus you probably did from the beginning. Several relationships with a partner finishes simply stops respecting the worth or feelings of the partner and comprise recent habits they ne'er would have done too soon.

For example, texting associates first love once you're married shouldn't happen. If you wouldn't expect a brand new date to be comfortable with that, why ought your significant other ignore it just because you're married?

Treat your partner with the utmost respect. try to make them smile. build an endeavor to schedule quality time shared between the 2 of you.

Date one another notwithstanding however long you've been along.

Never lose sight of how necessary trust is to stay healthy. Once one or the opposite partner isn't trustworthy, doubt creeps into the link. you'll be able to build or repair loss trust by.

Being there for your partner, each physically and showing emotion

Being consistent in your actions

Showing up after you say you'll

Keeping confidences

Respecting your partner's personal boundaries

Doing what you say you'll do

Have mutual and separate interests.

You cannot expect another person to finish you or to be everything that you are just a unit. it's healthy to share interests and to additionally maintain some activities you are doing apart. Once you enter into a partnership you become a team however every part of the team can gain one thing from additionally taking time to be private.

A relationship ought to enable you to be your core self, whereas providing you with somebody to like and love. it'll not be sensible for you or your partner if one amongst you becomes codependent ANd needs the opposite to require an interest in something.

Support one another's passions and dreams.

Support these dreams and additionally acknowledge you can't create all of them come back true. you're there to like and encourage their dreams, to not take responsibility for achieving them.[16]

While the 2 of you ought to have separate dreams, it can even be unifying to own shared goals that you just work towards as a team. Have a chat together with your partner and brainstorm some dreams you'd wish to accomplish along. It may be brought just by stating "I suppose it would be nice if we tend to set some shared goals. What area do we work towards together?"

CONCLUSION

Make sure you keep to all your promises.
Women don't like a man who can provide for their needs or who will promise but not fulfill, don't be too quick to judge them.

www.ingramcontent.com/pod-product-compliance
Lightning Source LLC
LaVergne TN
LVHW052117160826
845678LV00015B/3599
* 9 7 9 8 3 5 2 2 7 5 1 3 9 *